Astronaut Sally Ride talks to the ground control center at the Johnson Space Center from the flight deck of the earth-orbiting *Challenger* space shuttle.

SALLY RIDE, ASTRONAUT

An American First

By June Behrens

 CHILDRENS PRESS, CHICAGO

Acknowledgments

The author wishes to acknowledge with thanks the assistance of Dr. Dale Ride and Tony Baratta in the preparation of the manuscript.

Photo credits
  Dale Ride
  NASA
  Headmaster Nathan Reynolds,
    Westlake School For Girls

To Tom Kovach

Library of Congress Cataloging in Publication Data

Behrens, June.
  Sally Ride, astronaut.

  Summary: A biography of the California astrophysicist who became, with the second mission of the Challenger spacecraft in June of 1983, the first American woman and the youngest American astronaut to orbit the earth.
  1. Ride, Sally.   2. Astronauts — United States — Biography — Juvenile literature.   [1. Ride, Sally.   2. Astronauts]   I. Title.
TL789.85.R53B44   1984   629.45'0092'4 [B] [92]   83-23173
ISBN 0-516-03606-8

10 R 93 92

SALLY RIDE, ASTRONAUT
An American First

Sally checks on one of the experiments that was conducted while the *Challenger* was orbiting the earth.

4...3...2...1...0...Lift-off!

The rocket engines roar as *Challenger* leaves the launchpad. Over half a million people are at Cape Canaveral, Florida, to watch. In less than three minutes the spacecraft is thirty miles up. Soon it disappears from sight.

This is the second flight of *Challenger.* It carries a crew of five. Aboard is mission specialist Sally Ride, age thirty-two. She is a pioneer, the first American woman in space. Sally Ride is also the youngest American astronaut to circle the earth in a spacecraft.

Front row: Sally Ride, Robert L. Crippen (crew commander), Frederick (Rick) H. Hauck (pilot)
Second row: John M. Fabian and Norman E. Thagard

On the flight deck Sally Ride sits in the middle seat. She is just behind Commander Robert Crippin and Pilot Rick Hauck. Mission specialists John Fabian and Dr. Norman Thagard are also in their places. These astronauts are a team with an important mission.

The spacecraft is in orbit minutes after lift-off. *Challenger* orbits, or travels once around the earth, every ninety minutes. In one day the space crew orbits the earth sixteen times.

There is important work to do aboard the spacecraft. The astronaut

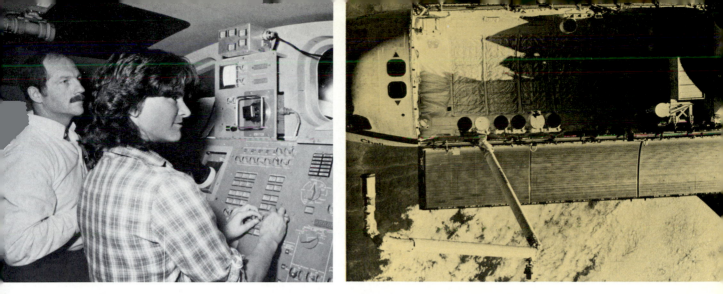

Sally Ride and Rick Hauck use the remote-control system that operates the robot arm. Through the windows the astronauts can look into the shuttle's cargo bay and watch the robot arm.

team runs scientific experiments. Two satellites are put into orbit. Astronaut Sally Ride works a fifty-foot robot arm. This is the first time it has been used in space. On future missions the robot arm will pick up satellites in trouble and repair them. Then the arm will return them to space.

The five astronauts complete their mission in six days. They have traveled 2.5 million miles. They return to earth, landing on the Mohave Desert in California.

Sally and her younger sister Karen (left).
Sally was on the Basketball A team in high school.

About one hundred miles from the
Mohave Desert is the town of Encino.
Sally Ride and her younger sister
Karen, nicknamed "Bear," grew up in
Encino. Her parents, Dale and Joyce
Ride, live there. Dr. Ride is an
educator, the assistant to the
president and superintendent at Santa
Monica College. Mrs. Ride was a
teacher at one time.

Sally knew she could do anything she wanted to do when she was a little girl growing up in Encino. Sally believed in herself. She had the will of a winner in school and in sports.

The neighborhood boys knew they'd have stiff competition in their baseball and football games when Sally was on the field. She was as good as any of them. Sally worked and played to make her team the best.

Sally was nine when Dr. Ride took a leave from his work in the schools. For a year the family traveled in Europe. Sally and her sister "Bear," aged seven, saw just how big the world is. What a great adventure, learning about other people in other countries!

In the Westlake School for Girls A-team tennis photo (above), Sally is the fifth from the right.

After the family came home from Europe, Sally took up tennis. She knew that a winner must work hard.

Sally worked hard and played hard on the tennis court. She became the eighteenth ranked junior player in the United States. Sally worked just as hard in the classroom. She was determined to do her best in whatever she tried.

Sally (lying down in foreground of the photo) was in an honors program. She was a year younger than her classmates.

Sally Ride went to high school at Westlake School for Girls. She was one of the top six in her graduating class and a year younger than her classmates.

Sally Ride's favorite subject was science. She remembers her science teacher as an important influence in her life.

In college Sally studied the science of stars and planets called astrophysics. She was interested in great books and literature. Sally was graduated from Stanford University with two degrees, one in English and one in astrophysics.

Sally Ride continued her studies. At Stanford University she earned the master's and doctoral degrees in astrophysics. She was now Dr. Sally Ride.

One day at school Sally Ride saw an ad in a newspaper. Men and women were wanted for the space program. They would be trained to become astronauts.

Sally was a research assistant in the physics department at Stanford University when she was selected for the astronaut training program.

Sally Ride was one of 8,900 people who wanted to be in the NASA astronaut training program. NASA is short for National Aeronautics and Space Administration. NASA looked for winners, people who were the best in their fields. Just 35 of the 8,900 applicants were chosen for the NASA astronaut class of 1978. Sally Ride was one of the six women chosen.

Sally Ride moved from her school
in California to the Johnson Space
Center in Houston, Texas. This is the
control center for NASA spacecraft
missions and astronaut training
programs.

Sally learned to fly jets. In a simulation exercise (left) at survival school, she learned how it feels when the pilot's seat is ejected out of a jet.

Before she knew it, Sally Ride was back in the classroom again. Her classes were in basic astronaut training. She had to know all about computer systems and the hundreds of switches that control a spacecraft. In space shuttle training she practiced spacecraft launching and entry. Sally Ride became a flight engineer and a pilot.

During on-the-ground training exercises Sally watched the robot arm move cargo in and out of the shuttle's cargo bay through the overhead window.

The training was hard work, physically and mentally. Sally Ride spent two years developing and working with the robot arm, which would be used on the spacecraft.

To keep fit Sally played softball, volleyball, and team games with her fellow astronauts. She liked to fly a small airplane. She jogged several times a week.

The astronaut training program includes parachute training, operating the *Challenger*'s complex controls in simulated exercises, and fire fighting exercises.

Sally posed with her father, mother, sister, and brother-in-law before her space shuttle adventure.

In the astronaut training classes Sally met astronaut Dr. Steven Hawley. They worked together and were interested in the same things. Sally Ride and Steven Hawley were married on July 24, 1982. Two ministers performed the ceremony— Dr. Bernard Hawley, father of the groom, and Karen "Bear" Ride, sister of the bride.

When astronaut Joe Engle and Richard Tully flew the space shuttle *Columbia* in earth orbit, Sally served on the mission control team at the Johnson Space Center in Houston.

Sally Ride served twice as a capsule communicator at Mission Operations Control Center in Houston. A capsule communicator talks and relays instructions to astronauts in orbit on space flights.

A pre-set camera captured this shot of all five crew members in space.
From left to right are astronauts Thagard, Crippen, Hauck, Ride, and Fabian.
There is no pull of gravity in space. You can see how Sally's necklace
seems to float around her neck.

The best-qualified people were
chosen for the second *Challenger*
mission. NASA officials wanted team
players, people who could work well
together. Sally Ride would be a
member of that team.

Sally and Karen Ride

Sally Ride came back to Encino to
visit her family. Her sister "Bear"
came home, too. Dr. and Mrs. Ride
were very proud of their daughters.
One was an astronaut and one was a
minister to the church.

A camera on an unmanned, free-flying shuttle satellite photographed the *Challenger* with its cargo bay empty. Later, using the robot arm, Sally retrieved a satellite from space and moved it into the cargo bay for its return to earth.

They remembered those early travels in faraway countries. Soon Sally would be looking down at the earth from 185 miles in space. She would be passing over those countries of the world ninety-six times.

24

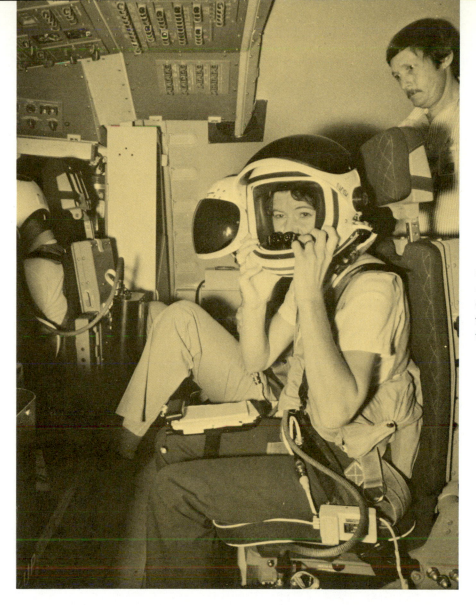

In simulators the crew went through every step of the *Challenger's* flight from take off to landing.

Back at Houston Sally Ride and her team worked to make the mission a success. They did in training all the things they would be doing as their spacecraft orbited the earth.

Astronauts Terry J. Hart and Sally Ride practice using the robot arm (above). In water survival training (right), Sally was dropped into the water from a moving boat. Then she had to learn to release herself from her parachute harness while being dragged by the boat. Sally Ride and John Fabian (opposite page) take a mission test. Only the best astronauts could be part of the *Challenger*'s team.

Rockets blast the *Challenger* into orbit.

When *Challenger* lifted off the pad at Kennedy Space Center in Cape Canaveral, the world watched. Everyone listened as the astronaut team reported activities to Mission Control in Houston.

The *Challenger* glided to a safe landing at Edwards Air Force Base in southern California.

Six days later, *Challenger*'s second mission touched down to a happy landing on the California desert. Sally Ride had made history. She had become the first American woman to orbit the earth. Her determination and hard work had made her a part of the winning team.

Astronauts Hauck, Thagard, Ride, and Fabian (far right) prepare a meal aboard the *Challenger*.

"The thing that I'll remember most about the flight is that it was fun," said Sally Ride. "In fact, I'm sure it was the most fun that I will ever have in my life."

SALLY KRISTEN RIDE

1951	Born May 26 in Los Angeles, California, daughter of Dale and Joyce Ride
1968	Graduated from Westlake School for Girls, Los Angeles, California
1969	Attended Swarthmore College; winner, intercollegiate tennis tournament; nationally ranked eighteenth among U.S. eighteen-year-olds
1973	Graduated from Stanford University with degrees in English and astrophysics
1978	Received Ph.D. in astrophysics from Stanford University; selected as one of thirty-five for NASA astronaut training program
1982	Selected to be the first American woman in space; July 24 — married fellow astronaut Dr. Steven Hawley
1983	June 18 — launch of the second flight of *Challenger* with mission specialist Sally Ride aboard; June 24 — return to earth after six days in orbit

JUNE BEHRENS has written more than fifty books, plays, and filmstrips for young people, touching on all subject areas of the school curriculum. Mrs. Behrens has for many years been an educator in one of California's largest public school systems. She is a graduate of the University of California at Santa Barbara and has a Master's degree from the University of Southern California. Mrs. Behrens is listed in Who's Who of American Women. She is a recipient of the Distinguished Alumni Award from the University of California for her contributions in the field of education. She and her husband live in Rancho Palos Verdes, a Southern California suburb.